To

_____

From

_____

EVERYDAY GRACE

FOR MEN

60 DEVOTIONS

Ellie
Claire
gift & paper expressions

Ellie Claire® Gift & Paper Expressions
EllieClaire.com
Ellie Claire is a registered trademark of Worthy Media, Inc.

Everyday Grace for Men
Copyright © 2018 by Ellie Claire
Published by Ellie Claire, an imprint of Worthy Publishing Group, a division of Worthy
Media, Inc., One Franklin Park, 6100 Tower Circle, Suite 210, Franklin, TN 37067.

ISBN: 978-1-63326-194-5

Stock or custom editions of Ellie Claire titles may be purchased in bulk for educational,
business, ministry, fundraising, or sales promotional use. For information, please
e-mail info@EllieClaire.com.

For foreign and subsidiary rights, contact rights@worthypublishing.com

Cover by Jeff Jansen | AestheticSoup.net
Art by Istock.com
Typesetting by Bart Dawson

Contributing writers: George Bowers, Larry Dugger, Todd Gerelds, Carlton Hughes,
David McCracken, Dean T. Skoglund

Printed in China
2 3 4 5 6 7 HAHA 22 21 20 19 18

*F*aith is a living, daring confidence

in God's grace, so sure and certain

that a man could stake

his life on it a thousand times.

MARTIN LUTHER

Of Apples and Talents

*Having then gifts differing according to the grace
that is given to us, let us use them.*

ROMANS 12:6 NKJV

When my wife and I bought our house many years ago, we inherited two apple trees in the backyard and had no idea how to care for them. The first season, the two trees yielded an abundance of good apples, but the following year they produced nothing. I consulted a friend, who explained the necessity of pruning the branches to ensure a good harvest of fruit the next year. I tried the technique, but I have come to realize that I simply do not possess a green thumb!

Recently, as I navigated the obstacle course of knobby apples in our yard, I said a quick prayer of repentance for the wasted fruit strewn across the ground and for my lack of attention to our trees. As I contemplated the unkempt fruit trees, I realized that my experience with them is similar to the talents and gifts the Lord has given me. I try to cultivate them as God intended, but in some cases I have neglected those gifts until they, too, resemble rotten apples and overgrown tree branches.

Thankfully, God knows me and understands my habits. He is patient with me when I choose to play

Solitaire instead of preparing my Bible study lessons. I am not defending my slackness, but rather appreciating that God is faithful to me even when I neglect my responsibilities. He understands my humanness and loves me anyway . . . and that's what I call grace.

Lord, help me use the talents and gifts You have blessed me with and not neglect them.

It has been my observation that the happiest of people, the vibrant doers of the world, are almost always those who are using—who are putting into play, calling upon, depending upon—the greatest number of their God-given talents and capabilities.

JOHN GLENN

The Next Big Thing

*Rejoice always, pray continually,
give thanks in all circumstances;
for this is God's will for you in Christ Jesus.*

1 THESSALONIANS 5:16–18 NIV

From childhood, many of us developed a habit that can cause us to miss God's presence in our lives. We conditioned ourselves to *look forward* to the "next big thing": the weekend, our birthday, Christmas, summer break, a first date, our first car, graduation, a new job, a vacation, marriage, children, and retirement. While there is nothing inherently wrong with anticipating life's next big event, being too fixated on tomorrow can cause us to miss the importance of the moment at hand.

The Bible teaches us that we are "created in Christ Jesus to do good works, which God prepared in advance for us to do" (Ephesians 2:10 NIV). This means that God is at work around us and through us, and we may not even be aware of it! God desires that we see Him in creation. He desires that we find joy in Him. But doing this comes easiest when we learn to find contentment in wherever He has us right now. He is with us in every moment and in each circumstance. And He desires that we see His hand in whatever He has given us to do right now. When we learn to be present in the presence of God, like Paul we will find contentment and joy in what we may have otherwise considered life's mundane moments.

Father, I ask that You would give me spiritual eyes to see You at work in my day-to-day activities. Help me turn my eyes from the next big thing and learn to find contentment, peace, and joy as I trust You with this present moment.

Listen to your life. See it for the fathomless mystery that it is. In the boredom and pain of it no less than in the excitement and gladness: touch, taste, smell your way to the holy and hidden heart of it, because in the last analysis all moments are key moments, and life itself is grace.

FREDERICK BUECHNER

Delayed by Grace

*Wait on the LORD; be of good courage,
and He shall strengthen your heart;
wait, I say, on the LORD!*

PSALM 27:14 NKJV

Today I was driving home from work on a narrow country road and found myself behind a huge tractor trailer. It was travelling at half speed, and every time there was a passing lane, either another car was coming at us or the tractor trailer sped up. Patience is not one of my virtues, and I was anxious to get home after a stressful day. As the miles passed, my frustration grew.

Eventually there was a catch in my spirit. I began to wonder if my delay behind this truck wasn't actually a moment of grace. Our sovereign God knows and sees everything, so maybe He allowed this delay to save me from something: an accident, a drunk driver, or maybe even a deer or a bear crossing the road into the path of my vehicle. Who knows what could have happened on this treacherous road?

God knew. After I thanked God for the delay, I breathed easier and took in the sights of the slow, scenic ride. How often has God's unseen hand protected me from danger without me even knowing it? How many times have I prayed for something and become upset when I had to wait for the answer? As impatient as I can be, I have learned to be thankful for God's grace that comes through the delays and small inconveniences in life. When we learn to operate in God's timing, we can sit back and enjoy the ride.

Lord, make me aware of Your unseen hand protecting and guiding me even when I am impatient.

The keys to patience are acceptance and faith.
Accept things as they are, and look realistically
at the world around you. Have faith in yourself
and in the direction you have chosen.

RALPH MARSTON

Campfires
and Communion

When [the disciples] got there,
they found breakfast waiting for them—fish cooking
over a charcoal fire, and some bread.
"Bring some of the fish you've just caught," Jesus said.

JOHN 21:9–10 NLT

A friend recently held a reunion at his farm for the staff members of our previous employer. His land is beautiful and peaceful, and the mile-long driveway, no more than a gravel path really, meanders through some rolling Tennessee countryside before it comes to an end facing a large barn.

It was good to spend a perfect early fall day in an open field surrounded by familiar faces and new friends. After an afternoon of great fellowship, a few tosses of the football, and way too much food, the crowd began to dissipate, until only a handful of us were left. The sun was just beginning to set when our host lit a bonfire and picked up his guitar. We sat around the fire well into the morning as we recounted old memories and made a few new ones between songs.

Our host shared a story of the previous autumn when a group of his friends sat in the same circle of chairs that we now occupied and enjoyed the time together so much that they decided to keep the fire going for as many days as possible. At the time, none of them seemed to know exactly why it was important to maintain the fire, but it somehow became a priority for each of them.

Some chose to come stoke the fire alone at night for the starry solitude. Others brought a friend or two so that they could spend a day together and share a campfire meal. One guy brought each of his kids separately for a camp night with their dad. There were encounters with wildlife . . . a midnight visit from a skunk, the sound of nearby coyotes making a kill, the clatter of night birds. They kept the fire going for weeks, and it made everyone feel as if they were part of something extraordinary.

As I left the farm that evening, I was acutely aware of the campfire as a metaphor for the church. It is a place where we gather to celebrate and share life together. It is the source from which we love our neighbors and keep God's extraordinary work burning bright with warmth and invitation to a world in darkness.

Jesus, just as You knew the value of gathering friends around a campfire for food and fellowship, help me find creative ways of building and strengthening relationships with the people I care most about.

Who has smelled the woodsmoke at twilight,
who has seen the campfire burning,
who is quick to read the noises of the night?

RUDYARD KIPLING

A Light to My Path

Your word is a lamp to my feet
and a light to my path.

PSALMS 119:105 ESV

A flashlight in a dark, wooded area keeps us from stumbling. Years ago, in a hurry to get to a campfire, I neglected to use that light and tripped on a root that I couldn't see in the dark. I scraped my arms and legs in my fall. The next morning I could clearly see the root on the path that bloodied my limbs.

While in India, a taxi driver taking me to my hotel had to stop in the middle of the road in a country area with no lights, no houses, and no way to call. I became alarmed and frightened. I was assured that someone would come help us, but that did not calm my fears. I had no idea where I was or where I could go for assistance. Furthermore, I could not see anything in the dark. Fortunately, another car appeared, its lights cutting through the darkness to help us.

From a spiritual standpoint, our world is portrayed biblically as existing in a state of darkness. Jesus calls us to "let your light shine before others, so that they may see" (Matthew 5:16 ESV). In a dark, frightful, and uncertain world, nothing can quench the uncertainty of people like pure light. We have the tools and the ability to shine that light into the world so that others can see and be safe.

The Bible is the source of that light illuminating the darkness. It is the lamp that shows us what is ahead and helps us see how to change course when our path is blocked. The Bible can give us guidance and comfort in difficult times. It helps us in our journey and can equip us to assist others along the way. So turn on that light! Dispel the darkness! Open your Bible today!

Father, teach me to use Your Word as a guide to shine light upon my journey. Give me insight to shine Your truth so others can see a clear path to walk.

*Darkness cannot drive out darkness;
only light can do that.*

MARTIN LUTHER KING JR.

Our Place
in God's Woods

*You are the body of Christ,
and each one of you is a part of it.*

1 CORINTHIANS 12:27 NIV

As you stroll through the autumn woodlands, the leaves of many trees decorate the landscape. The rich red maples, the bright yellow hickories, and the occasional orange of a sassafras combine for a beautiful display. The almost endless species of oak complement the color scheme and add their own hues to the living canvas.

Most eastern forests are made up of many species of trees. Although they vary in height, diameter, leaf shape, and bark design, God made them each for a reason. Aside from their beautiful fall display, maples provide sap for syrup and wood for cabinets. The sassafras provides delightful flavor for drinks and candies, while ash trees yield some of the best baseball bats on the diamond. Hickories contribute tool handles and barrel staves as well as tasty wildlife treats. Oaks, however, are the most versatile: they supply flooring, firewood, and furniture for humans and an abundance of acorns for critters. Every tree in God's creation has a unique place and a purpose.

And so does every man. Each of us is different from the rest, but God has designed every one of us to thrive in a particular environment and to contribute to the world around us. Some of us may be better at sales, others are exceptional teachers, while still others are gifted with their hands. It may take us some time to find the niche God has designed us for, but we each have a unique place and purpose. With the direction of the Holy Spirit and the encouragement and advice of others we, too, can become part of God's forest of color.

Father, reveal Your niche for me, and help me thrive there.

You are a unique blend of talents, skills, and gifts, which makes you an indispensable member of the body of Christ.

CHARLES STANLEY

Perfectly Weak

He said to me, "My grace is sufficient for you,
for My strength is made perfect in weakness."

2 CORINTHIANS 12:9 NKJV

Most men want to be thought of as strong, right? That is why we sometimes stand in front of the mirror flexing. Yes, it's okay to admit it! You're in good company. We've all done it at least once. I know I have. After all, no man wants to be thought of as a weakling.

However, in regard to our relationship with God, what if we have that backward? Is God looking for strong men? I guess that depends upon your definition of strong.

Does it ever seem like God is nearest to the spiritual giants? The ones who are exceptionally gifted and are right there on the front lines fighting the Lord's battles? Maybe someone like Billy Graham comes to mind when you picture one of God's "heavy lifters." But according to the scripture, it's not our *strength* that brings God the closest—it's our *weakness*. Jesus was always leaving the company of the strong to spend time with those who had little or no strength left. Powerlessness attracted Him.

If you feel weak, take heart! It means God is near. Remember that His strength is what always carries you through. Your humble admission of weakness pulls God away from His throne room to come near and sit with you in your living room. Your weakness is an opportunity for God to show His strength. Your admission of powerlessness is actually His invitation . . . so invite Him in today!

Dear God, help me be strong in the power of Your might.

When your power ends,
God's power is only beginning.
When you are weak
that is when He is strong in you!

VICTORIA OSTEEN

*Gratitude is what we radiate
when we experience grace,
and the soul was made to run on grace
the way a 747 runs on rocket fuel.*

JOHN ORTBERG

A Pause from Productivity

Seek first his kingdom and his righteousness,
and all these things will be given to you as well.

MATTHEW 6:33 NIV

Most men are driven to succeed. We like to accomplish things at work, at home, on the field, and even at church. We often spend large amounts of time on our primary pursuits in an attempt to ensure our successes and avoid failures.

While we should be concerned about our work ethic and the quality of our products, realizing that success is ultimately a gift from God brings greater appreciation for a job well done—a job well done in His strength. If we seek Him and His kingdom first, He has promised to provide our necessities. Thankfully, He often delivers far beyond our minimum requirements and showers us with many undeserved blessings. This truth is sometimes difficult for us to grasp, as we want to secure our own futures and reputations and labor tirelessly to do so.

When our highest priority is our relationship with God, from that foundational focus all else will flow: marriage, family, job, and the rest of life. If we neglect this vital component, even while working harder and harder, we choke off the very source of our life, and whatever perceived successes we may enjoy will become meaningless.

Even though it seems counterintuitive, when we pause from our work and take the time to maintain a close relationship with our Father, we are able to discover His will and a door is opened for His peace, joy, and blessing to enter our lives. Take some time each day to seek the Lord and to enjoy His precious presence.

Father, forgive me of my busyness, and may I reserve time to spend with You daily.

Lord, you establish peace for us;
all that we have accomplished you have done for us.

ISAIAH 26:12 NIV

Can You Hear Me Now?

Behold, I will stand before you there on the rock . . .
and you shall strike the rock,
and water shall come out of it.

EXODUS 17:6 ESV

Obedience means listening and doing exactly what we are told to do. God told Moses to *strike* a rock for water. In another instance, God told Moses to simply *speak* to the rock, but Moses disobeyed God by striking the rock instead (like he had some success doing before). And "because you did not believe in me" (Numbers 20:12), Moses was not allowed to go into the land that God had given to Israel. What God truly desires from us is that we learn to obey Him and His Word.

Rather than listen to Him, we often prefer to do things *our* way, because we have developed habits and we think our way is easier. We don't embrace change. Sometimes we are like Moses and choose *our* way because we don't want to fail. If it worked in the past, it will work again, right?

It's comforting to remember that Moses was not always obedient, and there were consequences to his disobedience. But true, more gratifying success comes when we focus on pleasing God and doing what He wants rather than what we want.

God wants to create new adventures and to vary our journey and excite us with new patterns of living because He knows that is how we grow.

When we come in search of life's sustaining waters, He wants us to depend upon His way rather than our way. And most times His way cannot be found when we're trying to do it on our own. "My sheep hear My voice, and I know them, and they follow Me" (John 10:27 NKJV). Are you listening for His voice? Let Him guide you.

Father, help me hear what You say. Help me learn to depend upon Your Word and not rely on my own ways and thoughts.

*I don't see success as the goal.
Obedience is the goal.*

JERRY B. JENKINS

Of Grace and Gravity

The purposes of a person's heart are deep waters,
but one who has insight draws them out.

PROVERBS 20:5 NIV

A buddy of mine has always loved roller coasters. Ever since he was big enough to ride the tallest, scariest, most-thrilling ones, they have been both an escape from the worst times of his life and a tangible way for him to celebrate the best times. After a difficult season of change and loss that left him feeling defeated, a group of his close friends surprised him with the gift of a solo road trip through three states to celebrate his upcoming birthday (one that was a significant life marker) with stops planned at every amusement park along the way to ride roller coasters.

This celebration journey was intended to provide my friend with the time to concentrate on recognizing both the grace and the gravity of life. My friend returned from his journey more aware that *embracing* the rhythms of everyday life, which are much like the peaks and valleys of a rollercoaster, can be the most thrilling ride of all. Time apart from his work and family reminded him that his greatest purpose is to praise God and love others no matter what circumstances life brings.

Even when life is at its most challenging, grace is found along the journey by trusting God through each moment of life's breathtaking rises and falls.

Father, thank You for providing us with a life full of possibilities and adventures at every turn! I am so grateful that You are with me in every high and through every low.

The only ones to get hurt on a roller coaster are the jumpers.

PAUL HARVEY

Mysterious Ways

*You intended to harm me, but God intended
it for good to accomplish what is now being done,
the saving of many lives.*

GENESIS 50:20 NIV

Joseph's story reveals God's power to work through circumstances that, from a human perspective, seem impossible. Joseph's brothers were jealous of him and planned to leave him to die in a well in the wilderness before ultimately selling him to merchants, who then sold him into slavery in Egypt. This act of jealousy and selfishness was a horrible evil against their brother. Nonetheless, God orchestrated circumstances to bring Joseph through slavery and imprisonment into a place where he could be used by God in an extraordinary way.

God gave Joseph particular gifts that enabled him to rise from slavery and prison to a position second only to Pharaoh. God showed Joseph that a devastating famine would come following several years of prosperity. This revelation allowed Joseph to set aside surplus grain during the years of plenty. When the famine came, Joseph's brothers traveled to Egypt to get grain for their family. While overseeing the distribution of grain, Joseph recognized his brothers. Though his brothers had intended him harm, and despite the resulting rough journey, Joseph saw that God had directed his path and was, therefore, able to graciously forgive his brothers. Joseph recognized that God works in mysterious ways.

God still works this way. Poverty, depression, job loss, difficult family circumstances, betrayal, and painful situations may come our way through no fault of our own. Stories from Joseph and others, including the story of the cross, show us that God can turn horrible events for good. Our God is a redeeming God.

Father, I pray that You will help me trust You with my circumstances. Help me recognize that even the worst situations can be a part of Your greater plan.

You can never change the past.
But by the grace of God, you can win the future.
So remember those things which will help you forward,
but forget those things which will only hold you back.

RICHARD C. WOODSOME

Just Keep Casting!

Simon answered, "Master, we've worked
hard all night and haven't caught anything.
But because you say so, I will let down the nets."
When they had done so, they caught
such a large number of fish
that their nets began to break.

LUKE 5:5–6 NIV

Apparently I have more in common with the disciples than I thought. I, too, have fished all night without catching anything. "Just one more cast," I've often told myself, hoping the next flip of the rod would produce my dinner. And way too often I have packed up and headed for home, exhausted and empty-handed.

Life can sometimes feel like a failed fishing trip. You've worked hard and given it your all, only to come up short. You've cast the vision, but no one was biting. I know that feeling so well because I have been there.

Fifteen publishers rejected my first book before it was finally picked up. Four years of blood, sweat, and tears just sat in the water without so much as a nibble. I wanted to quit at times, but instead, I kept casting (rewriting) and eventually I landed a contract.

Right before the miraculous catch, Jesus gave these instructions: "Put out into the deep water, and let down the nets for a catch" (Luke 5:4 NIV). The deepest part of the lake is where the fish were found. Trolling through the shallows wasn't going to fill the nets. When nothing is happening in your life, move toward deeper waters: deeper in prayer, deeper into the Word, and deeper into your commitment to your goal. Adjust the bait if you must, but just keep casting!

Dear God, help me launch out into the deep. Keep me fishing even when nothing seems to be biting.

The difference in winning and losing
is most often . . . not quitting.

WALT DISNEY

Who I Am

See what great love the Father has lavished on us,
that we should be called children of God!
And that is what we are!

1 JOHN 3:1 NIV

I was really excited when a friend of mine asked me to teach some sessions at a retreat in Colorado. I thought a 1,200-mile road trip would fuel my sense of adventure and the majesty of the Rockies would do much to energize my soul. As I prepared the lessons, another thought hit me: *I will have to make some sort of introduction to tell this group of people who I am.* Panic set in, and I actually contemplated canceling the whole trip!

Writing stories that invite readers into the lives of other people is something I relish; their lives seem so much more intriguing than my own. I'm not a husband or a father. I have lived in the same area all of my adult life, and my job doesn't reveal anything terribly interesting about my identity. I realized I needed a completely new perspective if I was going to share thoughts on my own journey. So I began by asking a very profound question: "Who does God say I am?" I picked up the Bible to do a little research and, man, oh man, was I humbled when I read my biography through the eyes of God:

I am God's child (Galatians 3:26). I am Jesus's friend (John 15:15). I am a whole new person with a whole new life (2 Corinthians 5:17). I am a place where God's Spirit lives (1 Corinthians 6:19). I am God's incredible work of art (Ephesians 2:10). I am totally and completely forgiven (1 John 1:19). I am created in God's likeness (Ephesians 4:24). I am spiritually alive (Ephesians 2:5). I am a citizen of heaven (Philippians 3:20). I am God's messenger to the world (Acts 1:8). I am God's disciple maker (Matthew 28:19). I am the salt of the earth (Matthew 5:13). I am the light of the world (Matthew 5:14). I am greatly loved (Romans 5:8).

Lord, thank You for giving me identity, value, and purpose. Whenever I feel adrift, or if others cause me to question my worth, I can rest assured that the truth of who I am is found in Your very Word.

It is difficult to make a man miserable while he feels worthy of himself and claims kindred to the great God who made him.

ABRAHAM LINCOLN

A New Creation

Be transformed by the renewal of your mind.

ROMANS 12:2 ESV

The word *transform* comes from the Greek word *metamorphoo* (or in English, *metamorphosis*). It is a change from what was to something new, different, and noticeable. Think of it in terms of the way a not-so-attractive caterpillar is changed into a beautiful butterfly.

Paul said we will be very different when we renew our mind in godly principles. It is a spiritual rebirth by the work of the Holy Spirit. We make a choice on our journey: we can stay as we are, or we can change and become someone new, better, and more beautiful.

Our parents squeezed us into a character they found desirable. Teachers and school peers reinforced or redirected us, as do friends, colleagues, professors, and employers who try to make us conform to their expectations. Paul stated that the world around us molds us in ways that are unsuitable and detrimental to us.

Paul wanted us to renew our minds as a process of transformation, changing us into a new creation (2 Corinthians 5:17). He suggested we refresh or restore our understanding of God's will and His purpose for our lives. It is our decision to be open to the transformative power of the Holy Spirit (John 14:16, 25–26).

Father, I ask that You renew my mind, change my behavior, and make me into a new, beautiful person so others can see Your work in my life.

The first step in conforming our intellect to God's truth
is to die to our vanity, pride, and craving
for respect from colleagues and the public.
We must let go of the worldly motivations that drive us,
praying to be motivated solely by a genuine desire
to submit our minds to God's Word—and then
to use that knowledge in service to others.

NANCY PEARCEY

The apostle Paul never seemed to exhaust the topic of grace—what makes us think we can? He just kept coming at it and coming at it from another angle. That's the thing about grace. It's like springtime. You can't put it in a single sentence definition, and you can't exhaust it.

MAX LUCADO

Rain, Rain, Go Away?

These things I have spoken to you,
that in Me you may have peace.
In the world you will have tribulation;
but be of good cheer, I have overcome the world.

JOHN 16:33 NKJV

Mʸ sons and I love to camp, and we always have unexpected adventures in the great outdoors. A few years ago, we decided to rough it at a nearby state park. It had been raining for days, with the forecast calling for even more of the wet stuff, but we forged ahead, getting our campsite set up even as the clouds rolled in. We searched for our tarp to cover the tent but realized we had forgotten it. My younger son stayed behind to guard our belongings while my older son and I went to town for a tarp. Just as we reached the store, the rain began to fall, and our phones lit up with texts.

"Get garbage bags!"

"Get a bucket!"

"Get a big tarp!"

"Hurry!"

A monsoon-like downpour hit the campground, and my son tried to empty out the rushing water as best he could, with his hands and with anything else he could find. But when we returned with supplies, something wonderful happened. Despite the gloomy forecast, the clouds parted and the sun shone bright, making the way for a rain-free evening. We dried out the tent and enjoyed our time together, engaging in fun card games and great conversation. We were all glad we had decided to ride out the stormy weather.

Do life's circumstances sometimes flood your life with little or no warning? Do you sometimes feel like you have little more than a spoon to clear out the water? You're not alone. Jesus warned that we would face trials and tribulations, but He also promised to be with us as we trudge through life's rainy seasons. His grace is enough to get us through to the sunshine that is always just on the other side of those storm clouds.

Lord, stay close to me as I navigate life's storms.

Life becomes inspiring, not in spite of the problems and the hard hits, but because of them.

JONI EARECKSON TADA

Living with Expectation

No, dear brothers and sisters, I have not achieved it,
but I focus on this one thing: Forgetting the past and
looking forward to what lies ahead, I press on to reach
the end of the race and receive the heavenly prize
for which God, through Christ Jesus, is calling us.

PHILIPPIANS 3:13–14 NLT

I recently had the privilege of coordinating an event honoring the much-beloved singer-songwriter Rich Mullins on the twentieth anniversary of his passing. About fifty of his family and friends gathered on a gorgeous fall day surrounded by acres of Tennessee farmland where the splendor of God's creation was an undeniable reminder of Rich's most well-known song, "Awesome God."

Many of those in attendance had not seen each other in several years, so it was especially good to gather and break bread with one another, sing a few a cappella hymns of praise, and share some cherished memories of Rich. Our morning was filled with lots of laughter mixed with a few bittersweet tears.

I asked Rich's youngest brother, David, a pastor with the heart of a shepherd, to share a few words with our small assemblage, and he used the opportunity to remind us all that it is good to look back and to remember well. But he also lovingly challenged us not to get stuck in memories of the past and allow them to prevent us from embracing those we love in the present and expecting God's new work in our lives.

Our service ended with a powerful communion ceremony that allowed both the beauty and the sting of David's message to be digested along with the elements that remind us of how much Jesus loves us. We left with a sense of peace that found us all more focused on looking ahead—living expectantly—rather than fixating on what has already passed.

Lord, I no longer want to be chained to my past. Please continue to build my faith in ways that allow me to confidently trust in the plans You have for my future.

Holding onto what was isn't healthy for what is.

HANNAH WHITALL SMITH

The Testimony
of the Rings

He has caused his wonders to be remembered.

PSALM 111:4 NIV

Many men enjoy the physical exercise involved in cutting firewood. Chainsaws and splitting mauls have a way of bringing out the effort and the sweat required for success. Not only does the exertion build muscle and strength, but it also yields visible results in the form of a neat stack of firewood ready for the deepest snows.

One of the obvious consequences of this activity is that it exposes the inner growth rings of the trees for inspection. These concentric circles reveal the tree's history year by year and can tell much about what that particular plant has experienced over its lifetime. Wider rings indicate lush times with plenty of nutrients and water, while tighter rings reveal more difficult growing seasons caused either by drought or by stiffer competition from surrounding trees. Some larger trees reveal a hundred years or more of climate information, and their rings are an abbreviated journal for each particular specimen.

Although our lives don't have rings, we should each look back occasionally to reflect on our past. When we do, we will notice seasons of life when times were good and flush, as well as tougher times when life was more difficult. This kind of personal reflection can help us see the hand of God caring for us through thick and thin. If we neglect this important discipline, we miss out on key insights of how God has bountifully blessed us, even when we were unaware, and how He has been with us through even the leanest of years.

Lord, help me recognize Your blessing and presence in all of my life.

Many, LORD my God, are the wonders
you have done, the things you planned for us.
None can compare with you.

PSALM 40:5 NIV

The Aroma of Jesus

*Everywhere we go, people breathe
in the exquisite fragrance. Because of Christ,
we give off a sweet scent rising to God,
which is recognized by those on the way of salvation.*

2 CORINTHIANS 2:15 MSG

I remember my first bottle of cologne. My dad gave it to me when I was twelve. "Brute 33. Splash it on and it will make you smell like a man," he said. I am not sure if it helped me with the ladies, but it sure did alert them to my presence. I think I practically baptized myself in it!

The Bible tells us that our new life in Christ also has a fragrance. It's the aroma of Jesus! But what does Jesus smell like? Perhaps your mind goes to the home of Lazarus, where his sister Mary took a pint of an expensive perfume and poured it on Jesus's feet (John 12:3). In my opinion, Mary wasn't trying to make Jesus smell better; she was demonstrating to those reclining at the table (and to us) what authentic worship looks like.

Today I am reminding myself that Jesus didn't smell like freshly laid carpet in a new church sanctuary. His aroma wasn't that of a fellowship hall packed with homemade pies and hot coffee. He didn't have that new-car smell or the aroma of a suit straight from the dry cleaners.

Jesus smelled like the dusty roads on which He walked, on His way to help those in need of miracles. He smelled like the dead that He raised and the sick that He healed. His fragrance was that of large crowds who followed Him for days without bathing. His scent was smoke from the campfire over which He cooked and served breakfast to His disciples. The aroma of help, hope, and healing clung to His garments.

Jesus invites you to take His fragrance to those you cross paths with today. You, too, can be a breath of fresh air!

Dear God, help me exude the sweet scent Jesus that is recognized by those on the way to salvation.

Make me a fragrance that smells like love.

CHRISTIAN DIOR

"It" Is Finished,
but You Are Not

When he had received the drink,
Jesus said, "It is finished." With that,
he bowed his head and gave up his spirit.

JOHN 19:30 NIV

Occasionally God will place a period in your life where you hoped He would place a comma. The story feels like it has ended, but you're still stuck in the chapter. Maybe you have lost a job or a relationship—or maybe "it" is the death of a friend or family member. Maybe you are stuck in disbelief and can't imagine how to move on. I'm sure that's how the disciples felt the day Jesus died. How could it be over? What about the future?

I, too, have experienced times in my life when "it" was finished . . . and so was I. The path forward in these desperate moments was blocked by fear and uncertainty. My heart and my head were full of questions for God, like, "What happens now and where do I go from here?" I've even said, "Where were You and why did You allow this?" What I didn't realize in those times was that with God there is truly no finish line. Each end is only the beginning of a brand-new journey! Jesus wasn't finished just because "it" (the redemption of mankind) was finished . . . and so it is with us!

When something comes to an end in your life, you keep going. Like Jesus, a brighter tomorrow depends upon it. Where you're heading can be better than where you've been if you will commit to the future. Jesus gave up His spirit, but He didn't give up—and neither can you. What you see as a crucifixion, God sees as an opportunity for resurrection. The end is never the end when you trust that God is continuing His good work in you.

Dear God, I place "it" in Your hands. Help me look forward, knowing that I am not finished. Help me trust Your plan for the future.

I know what I am doing. I have it all planned out—
plans to take care of you, not abandon you,
plans to give you the future you hope for.

JEREMIAH 29:11 MSG

God's Love
in the Little Things

The heavens proclaim the glory of God.
The skies display his craftsmanship.
Day after day they continue to speak;
night after night they make him known.

PSALM 19:1–2 NLT

There are times as men when we long to have a stronger sense of God's love, presence, and reality in our day-to-day life. The enemy seeks to distract us and convince us that the physical realm is the only true reality. But when we stop and gaze upon God's eternal Word and listen to His still, small voice, we remember the truth that He is real. He is here. He is with us. He is speaking to us *through* His physical world.

God, our Father, is the One who gave man his senses to experience the goodness in creation. Waking up in the morning to the sounds of birds chirping and the smell of coffee brewing is a simple reminder of the truth that God gave us ears to enjoy the songs of our feathered friends and noses to breathe in the aroma of a cup of coffee. In the summertime we feel sand between our toes as we walk on the beach and look out over the blue-green water of the ocean. God gave us a sense of touch and eyes to see evidences of His creative power and beauty. God's design is that His creation would ever direct our eyes back to His glory.

Father, thank You for showing Your love and personal care for me through creation. Help me see that every good thing I experience in this world is a gift from You.

Grace is something you can never get
but can only be given. There's no way to earn it
or deserve it or bring it about any more
than you can deserve the taste of raspberries
and cream or earn good looks. . . .
A good night's sleep is grace and so are good dreams.
Most tears are grace. The smell of rain is grace.
Somebody loving you is grace.

FREDERICK BUECHNER

Forgiveness
Is Supernatural

*Who is a God like you, who pardons sin
and forgives the transgression of the remnant
of his inheritance? You do not stay angry
forever but delight to show mercy.*

MICAH 7:18 NIV

Looking down from the cross at those who had nailed
Him there, Jesus spoke to His Father in heaven: "Father,
forgive them . . ." (Luke 23:34 NIV). A few days earlier
these same people were cheering as Jesus entered Jerusalem
as the long-prophesied King. In the preceding days, Jesus
wept over Jerusalem and their unwillingness to accept the
loving care of God through Him.

Micah tells us that God forgives and *delights* to show
mercy. Jesus deeply loved the people who betrayed Him.
This betrayal and rejection certainly added immense emotional pain to His physical suffering on the cross. Still, He
delighted to show mercy.

As men, we will all experience betrayal and rejection.
When our injuries come from loved ones, the hurt can
be deep. Men often resort to one of two responses when
they are wounded. These reactions have been termed
fight-or-flight responses. We often lash out or withdraw

when experiencing emotional distress inflicted by someone we care about. This is *natural*. But God is calling us to
respond *supernaturally*. How was Jesus able to freely forgive
people who murdered Him? The supernatural source of
Jesus's forgiveness is His limitless love for His children.
God is calling men to reject our *natural* inclination when
faced with hurt and to instead release those who hurt us
by forgiving them.

Father, help me truly release those who wrong me. Let me
reject the lies that try to convince me that revenge or with-
drawal will make me feel better. Help me walk away from
my *natural* responses and embrace the *supernatural* loving
forgiveness that comes from You.

*A*mong the most powerful of human experiences
is to give or to receive forgiveness. . . .
Forgiveness is a collapsing into the mystery of God
as totally unearned love, unmerited grace.
It is the final surrender to the humility and power
of a Divine Love and a Divine Lover.

RICHARD ROHR

Our huffing and puffing to impress God,

our scrambling for brownie points, our

thrashing about trying to fix

ourselves while hiding our pettiness

and wallowing in guilt, are nauseating

to God and are a flat out denial

of the gospel of grace.

BRENNAN MANNING

To Be Strong
and Courageous

*Be strong and courageous, for you will bring
the Israelites into the land I promised them on oath,
and I myself will be with you.*

DEUTERONOMY 31:23 NIV

At the end of the book of Deuteronomy, Moses had led God's people faithfully for forty years and would soon die—the time had come for a change in leadership. God had chosen Joshua to lead the people across the Jordan and into the promised land. I'm sure this circumstance was both difficult and freeing for Moses. On the one hand, he had to feel incredibly relieved to know that the responsibility of leadership would now be off his shoulders. But it also had to be bittersweet, allowing someone else to shepherd the people who were so close to his heart.

I am most often captivated by Joshua's role in this story. Can you imagine succeeding the man who had led a nation of people out of slavery? Joshua was chosen by God to be the new leader and had also been mentored by Moses for many years. I bet even with all of his preparation, he still had some hesitation and anxiety about his new role. Even though Joshua trusted in God, having sole responsibility for this vast nation of pilgrims was formidable indeed.

Any of us who has ever started a new job can easily relate to Joshua's situation. Although we may have excellent training, ample experience, and great references, taking the helm of a new position can be intimidating, especially if it involves management or supervision of others. On such occasions, remember God's words to Joshua recorded above. Sensing Joshua's anxiety, God reassured him of His help and His presence. May these same promises from God bring us courage as well!

Oh God, give me the strength to handle whatever assignment You give me.

Be strong and very courageous. Be careful to obey all the law my servant Moses gave you; do not turn from it to the right or to the left, that you may be successful wherever you go.

JOSHUA 1:7 NIV

To Float Like Iron

As one of them was cutting down a tree,
the iron axhead fell into the water.
"Oh no, my lord!" he cried out. "It was borrowed!"
The man of God asked, "Where did it fall?"
When they showed him the place, Elisha cut a stick
and threw it there, and made the iron float.

2 KINGS 6:5–6 NIV

I can sympathize with the man in this story. If you're like me, any time I borrow something, it ends up either broken or lost! I, too, have said, "Oh no, it was borrowed!" How about you? A trip to the hardware store isn't very exciting when you're only going to purchase for your buddy a brand-new version of whatever it was you destroyed or can't find.

In the story of Elisha, it was an iron ax head. Once off the handle, it sunk to the bottom. Apparently the water was deep and recovery was impossible. It definitely wasn't coming back under its own power. Iron simply doesn't float! But when the prophet of God found the place where it had sunk, a miracle occurred and the iron actually floated.

I can also identify with the piece of iron in this story. Sometimes, like that ax head, I have flown off the handle.

I bet you have, too, on occasion. I have also felt like I was trapped under deep waters looking up at the crushing weight and wondering how I could ever get back to the surface.

I think we have to begin our recovery by asking ourselves, "Where did I fall in?" Did you topple over into the deep water of addiction? Or maybe you fell in the pool of pride? I believe once you have pinpointed the location of your descent, the miracle can begin in your life: you can float too!

Dear God, when I feel I am drowning, help me face the moment where I flew off the handle. Allow me to accept the grace and forgiveness to float out of those deep waters.

When you feel you're drowning in life, don't worry. Your lifeguard walks on water.

ANONYMOUS

At Rest in Daddy's Arms

[There is] a time to embrace . . .

ECCLESIASTES 3:5 NIV

When my children were young, I took them hunting with me as often as I could. Although the additional noise and movement likely cost me game, I wouldn't trade the biggest buck or the largest turkey for the blessing of having them along.

On one particular November morning, my son accompanied me into the deer woods. Since I couldn't afford a tree stand, we sat on the frozen ground with only an inch of thermal to ward off the cold. At first we were both pretty chilly, so I reached out and pulled him close in a large embrace. Even though my teeth were still chattering, it wasn't long until I could tell he was fast asleep.

As I sat there enjoying this precious moment of closeness in God's amazing creation, it reminded me of how God must feel when we snuggle up close to Him. Far too often we resist His gentle invitation to rest in Him because of the myriad of tasks on our to-do lists. Sometimes our guilt and shame keep us away from His warm embrace. What rest and joy we must miss by frittering our time and lives away outside of His arms!

58

That morning I kept watch just in case a deer showed up, but I was also vigilant for any threat that might come near, as my son trusted me completely. It was a brief moment in fatherhood to remember and to cherish forever. Moments like that can remind us all to crawl up beside Abba Father and allow Him to love on us for a while.

Daddy, I need one of Your strong hugs today. Thank You for loving me.

The Spirit you received does not make you slaves,
so that you live in fear again; rather,
the Spirit you received brought about your adoption
to sonship. And by him we cry, "Abba, Father."
The Spirit himself testifies with our spirit
that we are God's children.

ROMANS 8:15–16 NIV

The Lasting Gift
of Friendship

*Let us consider one another in order
to stir up love and good works.*

HEBREWS 10:24 NKJV

For two years in college, I was fortunate to have a great roommate. Our dorm room was the size of a walk-in closet with a community bathroom down the hall. Many people in our building actually became enemies with their roommates, considering such cramped quarters, but we hit it off immediately. We respected each other's space and shared an academic major and a love of music, movies, and Doritos. (Confessional time: I did not respect his space when it came to the Doritos.) He helped me in my photography classes, and I taught him Appalachian culture and an appreciation for University of Kentucky basketball.

Thirty years have passed, but my college roommate and I still remain close even though we live two hundred miles from each other. Our phone conversations are lively, our texts are wacky, and our periodic visits are fun. It has been three decades since we lived together in that "cracker box," but it feels as if we have only been apart for a few days when we reunite for sporting events at our alma mater.

We hear a lot about female friendships, but it is important—and godly—for men to have strong friendships as well. Guys may not talk much about feelings or relationships, but we do enjoy discussing sports and snack foods. God knows how hard it is to walk this path of life alone, so He graces us with friends who show up at the right time. Some pals may only be with us for a season, while others remain for a lifetime. Jesus modeled male friendships through the interactions with His disciples, exhibiting love and guidance, and He wants us to offer up that same dose of grace through our own relationships.

Father, thank You for the gift of friendship. May I follow Your lead with the people You place in my life.

There is nothing on this earth more to be prized than true friendship.

THOMAS AQUINAS

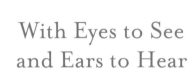

With Eyes to See
and Ears to Hear

You dwell in the midst of a rebellious house,
who have eyes to see, but see not, who have ears to hear,
but hear not, for they are a rebellious house.

EZEKIEL 12:2 ESV

We have eyes and ears, but we cannot understand (Proverbs 20:12). We are surrounded by the noise of rebellion on all sides, including from our jobs, the voices in the media, and even our own peers and relatives at times. When the truth comes to us, the noise around us can drown out the true message—unless we are intentional about finding quiet time with God.

Jesus often asked His disciples if they understood what He said. And even after three years of close contact, they did not recognize Him after His resurrection (Luke 24:16).

There are so many voices competing for our attention in today's world. All around us are voices shouting out what *they* believe is important. Our ears are constantly filled with differing viewpoints, and sometimes, if those voices are loud enough and persistent enough, we begin to believe them. We need a standard instruction to follow.

The Bible comprises our "Basic Instructions Before Leaving Earth." We have a guidebook to help us navigate our journey. It is our GPS to find our way through the treacherous noise of daily life. God has also given us the Holy Spirit, who will help us and direct us along the way (John 16:13). It is up to us to find the quiet in our day to fill ourselves with God's truth.

Father, teach me the importance of the Bible in my life and the need to quiet myself before You. Show me truth that I did not know, and help me change my ways as I more fully understand Your will for my life.

*Education is not the piling on of learning,
information, data, facts, skills, or abilities . . .
but is rather a making visible what is hidden as a seed . . .
To be educated . . . [is to be] exposed . . .
to the transformative events of an engaged human life.*

THOMAS MORE

The Power
of the Shortest Verse

Jesus wept.

JOHN 11:35 NIV

Jesus loved Lazarus and his sisters, Mary and Martha. Mary and Martha believed that Jesus could perform miracles. They sent word to Jesus that Lazarus had become sick. But Jesus delayed His return trip by two days, even knowing what the outcome would be. When He was ready to go, Jesus told the disciples that Lazarus had "fallen asleep" (John 11:11 NIV) and that He was going to wake him up. He was speaking figuratively, but they took Him literally. So He made it clear, "Lazarus is dead, and for your sake I am glad I was not there, so that you may believe. But let us go to him" (vv. 14–15 NIV).

At this point we realize that Jesus *knew* what He was going to do. He knew He was going to fix this terrible situation. Nonetheless, Jesus, with the knowledge, power, and desire to bring Lazarus back to life, to fix the situation, didn't . . . at least not in that moment. Jesus first came to the tomb amidst great sorrow and mourning from the people who loved Lazarus. The people's hearts were broken. Two words give us a glimpse into God's personal love for us and His emotion toward all of humanity: "Jesus wept."

These two words describe Jesus's response to hurting and grieving people. As a man, Jesus's response was perfect in every circumstance. Before He "fixed" the situation with Lazarus, it is vital for us to understand that He took time to be fully present with those people in the pain of loss and to grieve alongside them. As men, God calls us to love as Jesus loves, and He empowers us with His Spirit to do it. Men by nature tend to be "fixers." Jesus showed us that fixing things has its place, but sometimes love requires us to *feel* deeply as well.

Father, help me love as Jesus loves. Help me avoid my tendency to immediately try to fix everything. Instead, give me grace that I may be fully present with others when they are hurting.

Christ has put on our feelings along with our flesh.

JOHN CALVIN

The Goliath in My Mirror

*Put on the full armor of God,
so that you will be able to stand firm
against the schemes of the devil.*

EPHESIANS 6:11 NASB

I recently tried to purchase an authentic-looking "David slays Goliath" slingshot so I could use it to illustrate the Bible story for kids at my church. I searched every retail store in my town with no luck. Growing more and more frustrated, I decided I would attempt to make my own. I knew I would need some sinew threads, a piece of rawhide for the pouch, and some leather cord to make it really look the part.

A buddy of mine owns a leather store, so I decided to pay him a visit. His workshop is stacked from floor to ceiling with rolls, sheets, and pieces of every type, color, and scent of leather imaginable. When I told him about my project, he said he had everything I needed and he disappeared into the wilderness of his inventory.

On my excursion I had already been thinking about the young shepherd boy and the giant he faced, and as I admired the tools of the trade on my friend's work desk, I caught a glimpse of myself in the mirror on his office wall. I was struck with the realization that most of the giants

I confront are the ones I see in my own reflection. I reminded myself of the words the Holy Spirit has spoken to me on more than one occasion: "I want to see you face this giant. You are able and worthy." I imagined God whispering those exact same words to His faithful young servant as he stood in front of his mammoth foe.

Mighty God, You are a constant reminder that it only took one stone for David to defeat Goliath. Thank You for being my strength and for giving me the confidence I need to face my giants.

You know your Goliath. . . .
He taunts you with bills you can't pay,
people you can't please, habits you can't break,
failures you can't forget, and a future you can't face. . . .
David gives this reminder: Focus on giants—
you stumble. Focus on God—your giants tumble.

MAX LUCADO

When granted many years of life,
growing old in age is natural,
but growing old with grace is a choice.
Growing older with grace is possible
for all who will set their hearts
and minds on the Giver of grace,
the Lord Jesus Christ.

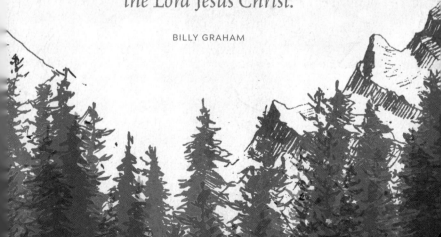

Confidence in the Storm

A furious squall came up, and the waves broke
over the boat, so that it was nearly swamped.
Jesus was in the stern, sleeping on a cushion.
The disciples woke him and said to him,
"Teacher, don't you care if we drown?" He got up,
rebuked the wind and said to the waves,
"Quiet! Be still!" Then the wind died down
and it was completely calm. He said to his disciples,
"Why are you so afraid? Do you still have no faith?"

MARK 4:37–40 NIV

According to the *Merriam-Webster Dictionary*, the phrase "ice water in one's veins" means "the ability to remain very calm and controlled in a situation in which other people would become upset or afraid." Sports fans often use this phrase to describe an athlete who comes through in "crunch time." The key to the athlete's calm is his self-confidence, self-awareness, and assurance that he will get the job done.

Jesus's self-awareness and assurance were absolute. He knew who He was. His disciples witnessed His ability to heal and to forgive sins. The teachers of the law who saw Jesus forgiving sins recognized He was claiming power that belonged to God alone. He then used His ability to heal the man He'd just forgiven to confirm that He was, *indeed*, God Almighty (Matthew 9:1–8). So when His disciples responded with fear to the storm they were encountering, Jesus questioned their faith because He'd had time and time again demonstrated that He was worthy of their trust.

Jesus's calming of that storm and His words to His disciples are instructive for us. When storms come, we have the ability to have that same calmness, not because of faith in our own power, but because of our relationship *to* and our confidence *in* Him.

Father, help me rest my confidence in You as I face the storms of life. Allow me to cast my cares upon You.

There are times, and there will be times, when it will be absolutely clear that only God's grace keeps us from falling apart; and even if we cannot hold on to Him, He will still hold on to us.

JOHANNES FACIUS

A Reflection
of My Father

*Long ago the LORD said to Israel: "I have loved you,
my people, with an everlasting love.
With unfailing love I have drawn you to myself."*

JEREMIAH 31:3 NLT

In the Garden, man's identity was found in his relationship with God. God's love and desire for a relationship with Adam tells us all we need to know about Adam's significance. The Creator of the universe designed Adam for the *purpose* of knowing God and being known by Him. When Adam decided he knew better than God and chose his own way, things changed. Scripture tells us that when Adam sinned, his eyes were opened and he immediately sought to cover himself (Genesis 3:7). He and his wife tried to hide from God in the very Garden He'd created for them to enjoy.

God created you for the same purpose He created Adam. God desires that you know Him and be known by Him. Through Jesus, God restored our ability to commune with Him. He has given His Spirit, who raised Jesus from the dead, to live *within* us, empowering us to live in submission to God and in communion with Him. Just as in the Garden, the enemy will lie to us, desiring that we do things our own way or that we try to hide behind the very gifts God has given us. Occupations, money, relationships, or any other things of this earth aren't meant to be the source of our identity or to shield us from our need of God. God desires that we glorify and reflect Him as we are stewards of the resources He has given us.

Father, thank You for establishing my identity through Christ and not through acquisitions, achievements, or accomplishments. Help me turn away from the temptation to find my significance anywhere except in Your love.

Look deep within yourself and recognize what brings life and grace into your heart. It is this that can be shared with those around you. You are loved by God. This is an inspiration to love.

CHRISTOPHER DE VINCK

Unless You Become
Like a Child

*Truly, I say to you, unless you turn
and become like children,
you will never enter the kingdom of heaven.*

MATTHEW 18:3 ESV

How do we become like a child when we are already grown up? That only comes from humbling ourselves and becoming completely dependent upon God. A child does not consider his status among others but depends upon others in good faith to meet his needs.

Pride and arrogance are natural to us because we want to take credit for what we do. We find our worth in the world by comparing ourselves to others. This causes us to become boastful, arrogant, and proud of our accomplishments. Jesus says that we enter the kingdom when we are like a child who does not know his significance or count it as important.

A child learns his worth from a parent just as we learn our worth from our heavenly Father. But when we find our significance from the people around us, we become dependent upon their approval, and that is always a recipe for failure and disappointment.

We can learn to depend upon God like a child by understanding our worth is grounded only in our relationship to Him. When we make the decision to depend upon Him for everything, then our significance is based only on what He says. We cannot enter into God's kingdom unless we begin to acknowledge that we are nothing apart from our relationship to God.

Father, help me understand the importance of depending upon You. Give me insight of Your grace for me. Help me focus on others rather than myself.

*Without God, life has no purpose,
and without purpose, life has no meaning.
Without meaning,
life has no significance or hope.*

RICK WARREN

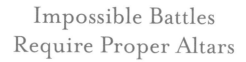

Impossible Battles
Require Proper Altars

Build a proper kind of altar to the LORD your God.

JUDGES 6:26 NIV

Was there a time in your life when it seemed as though there was nothing you could not face? Maybe there was a time when you felt like a heavyweight champion in your walk with God, but now you don't even feel like a contender.

Gideon's family had the same problems. Years of blessings quickly turned into misery once the wrong kind of altar was built. In Old Testament times, the altar was a powerful indicator of a person's priorities and focus: it identified *who* was being served or worshipped. The Israelites learned the hard way that an overcomer can become an underdog in a relatively short amount of time once focus is placed on the wrong things. In Judges 6, Gideon's father had built an altar to the false god named Baal—losing focus in a critical time when Israel's enemies were right at their doorstep. But Gideon followed God's command and was ultimately responsible for returning the proper focus back to the one true God, just as we are.

Ask yourself these two questions: Am I losing a battle because, like Israel, I have removed God from the center of my life? Is the altar of my life built for the one true God?

The size of Israel's adversaries was never Gideon's true problem. Rather, it was the condition of Israel's altar. Once Israel's altar to God was repaired, the enemy stood little chance. Gideon took a small group of three hundred men and defeated an enemy that was as numerous as the grains of sand on the seashore. The same can be true in your life. The things that once had power over you will quickly find they are no match for the almighty God living inside of you.

Dear God, today check the condition of my altar.

Moses built an altar and called it
The Lord is my Banner.

EXODUS 17:15 NIV

God's Extravagant Heart

Now to him who is able to do immeasurably more than all we ask or imagine, according to his power that is at work within us, to him be glory in the church and in Christ Jesus throughout all generations, for ever and ever! Amen.

EPHESIANS 3:20–21 NIV

On a beautiful December day, I enjoyed the special favor of God. While hunting at my favorite spot, I bagged the largest buck I had ever seen. It was a ten-point with a wide spread and tall tines. Although I'd put in the work to prepare, scouted the area beforehand, and spent many hours in that exact stand during bow and muzzle-loading seasons, I'd never seen that deer before. He was an extravagant gift that seemingly appeared out of nowhere that morning. It was a moment that made me reflect on the generous heart of God.

Most responsible adults do all we can to prepare for success. This is a key step of faithfulness—doing our part so that God might do His. We do this in our jobs, our hobbies, and our relationships. Completing our homework and developing plans are important steps that even biblical prophets and kings used to ensure achievement.

God empowers our work as we seek His direction and do our part. Sometimes, however, He goes much further than expected to bless us exceedingly, abundantly, beyond all we can ask or even imagine. The incredible blessing of a loving wife, the gift of healthy children, the trust of some measure of material wealth, and the opportunity to use our talents in gainful employment are all examples of God's gracious, generous heart. We may have made some preliminary preparations, but God gives us the increase!

Dear God, thank You for Your generous grace. Help me recognize it in my life.

Grace is God's free, spontaneous, unsolicited, even unreturned love, which finds its origin in itself, not in its object.

JOHN STOTT

Daddy, I Made a Mess

I know how bad I've been; my sins are staring me down.
You're the One I've violated, and you've seen . . .
the full extent of my evil. You have all the facts
before you; whatever you decide about me is fair.
I've been out of step with you for a long time.

PSALM 51:3–5 MSG

As the father of two boys, "Daddy, I made a mess" is a phrase with which I am very familiar. I heard it more times than I could count, and I'll admit I never looked forward to the ensuing investigation. An overflowing toilet or a broken jar of jelly often made the list of catastrophes. But boys make messes, and good dads let them know it's okay to admit to them so he can help with the cleanup.

In the same way, you have a heavenly Father, a divine Daddy, who is also good at cleaning up after you once you seek His help. He understands that you never outgrow your ability to sometimes make a real mess of things. While you no longer break jelly jars, you're capable of breaking people and inviting chaos because of poor choices.

David, the king of Israel and a man after God's own heart, also made some big messes. In his attempt to take care of it on his own, he usually made things far worse. Can you relate? I know I can. The *Merriam-Webster Dictionary* defines a *mess* using the following words: *shambles, chaos, trouble, dilemma,* and *problem.* No wonder my boys were always looking for me when they made one! Their first thought was, *Oh no, we need Daddy! He will know what to do!*

If you're in the middle of a mess, don't forget your Daddy (God). Your heavenly Father isn't excited that you messed up, but He will be happy that you included Him in the cleanup.

Dear heavenly Father, provide me the strength and the wisdom to come to You with my messes.

Soak me in your laundry and I'll come out clean, scrub me and I'll have a snow-white life.

PSALM 51:7 MSG

To Have the Mind of Christ

We have the mind of Christ!

1 CORINTHIANS 2:16 ESV

Paul established a principle for living the Christian life as having "the mind of Christ." We need to know the mind of Christ and practice it just as a child watches his father and imitates him. To follow Jesus means that we should observe Him as the disciples did and imitate Him in all we do.

We know and understand Jesus by the biblical account of His life and teachings. As we read about Him, we are to always ask, "What does it mean for me to practice that in my own life?" To become like Jesus is to do as He did (John 13:15). The more we understand and know Jesus, the more we will become like Him.

When Jesus left His disciples, they carried on His work. They had followed Jesus, learned from Him, and emulated Him. They realized they could meet the needs of people and help them connect to God in a relationship, just as Jesus had taught them.

Do you want to approach each new day with the *intent* to be like Jesus? That will only come more easily when we learn to pray, show kindness, love, and be concerned for others just as Jesus did. The Holy Spirit empowers us to do as Jesus did—to have *the mind of Christ*. That is what pleases God most.

Father, help me be intentional about following You. Help me show love and concern for someone today. Help me encourage another person in his journey.

Be imitators of me, as I am of Christ.

1 CORINTHIANS 11:1 ESV

*Grace is but glory begun,
and glory is but grace perfected.*

JONATHAN EDWARDS

Jesus Take the Wheel!

Where two or three gather in my name,
there am I with them.

MATTHEW 18:20 NIV

It was no surprise when my coworker walked into my office and said, "Can I ask a favor of you?" I assumed he was going to inquire about how to send a fax or where he might find a legal pad, so I was completely taken back when his follow-up question was, "Would you be willing to be my prayer partner?" I found myself saying yes, but as he walked away I thought, *What did he just ask and what did I just commit to?*

Over the next several days, doubts started to creep in as I began to question why he had chosen me. I wondered what would happen if we had spiritual differences or if he changed his mind because he thought I wasn't "good enough." What if his observation of my behavior in the office had led him to believe that I was in need of salvation?

Despite my initial insecurities, the morning of our first scheduled prayer time finally arrived, and we had to scramble for a creative solution as we realized there was no place for privacy in our filled-to-capacity office space. I half-jokingly suggested we use the company van and, after a moment of shared laughter, out to the parking lot we went. As we settled in and began to talk, I asked him why he had offered me this opportunity. Without hesitation he said, "Because I see Jesus in you."

So our weekly prayer time has occurred in the company van for months now, and we have yet to miss a single one. Usually we start by sharing what's going on in our own lives, and then we ask God to open our eyes to the needs of the people we work with so that we can effectively pray for them. Our time together has drawn us closer, and it has transformed the way I perceive my fellow employees. It has also given me the grace to see beyond my insecurities and focus on the strength of Jesus living in me.

Lord, thank You for blessing the time I spend in prayer as you constantly reveal things about who You are . . . and about who I am. You are an endless source of amazement and surprise.

We think of prayer as a preparation for work, or a calm after having done work, whereas prayer is the essential work. It is the supreme activity of everything that is noblest in our personality.

OSWALD CHAMBERS

The Threads
That Bind Us

You created my inmost being;
you knit me together in my mother's womb.

PSALM 139:13 NIV

I recently bought an Irish sweater, and the intricate pattern of stitches and knots created by its woven woolen threads made me think of a late beloved friend who fully embraced the Celtic ancestry we both share. I looked forward not only to its cozy comfort but also to the reconnection to memories of my friend that wearing the sweater would bring. But the weather was unseasonably warm that year, and it looked as if I would have to pack away any possibility of the physical and emotional warmth I might experience from the sweater and trust in that ecclesiastical promise that says, "To everything there is a season . . ." (Ecclesiastes 3:1 NKJV).

When a sudden thirty-degree drop in the temperature occurred, I was grateful for an opportunity to wear it out to a new neighborhood coffee shop where the barista noticed that my sweater originated from her home country. As we talked of our shared heritage and of the deliciousness of locally roasted coffee, I was struck by how her recognition of the patterns in the strands of my sweater had instigated the newfound commonalities and bound two total strangers together for a moment.

I left the coffee shop warmed by the brew and comforted by the image of God as the Master Weaver. The creative way He thoughtfully designs the threads of each of our lives into a unique creation and intertwines them with the lives of others makes our lives and endless source of surprise and wonder.

Lord, thank You for making divine connections in our lives. We are grateful that You bless us with these threads that bind us together and provide opportunities to know one another and to be known.

We look at life from the backside of the tapestry. And most of the time, what we see is loose threads, tangled knots and the like. But occasionally, God's light shines through the tapestry, and we get a glimpse of the larger design with God weaving together the darks and lights of existence.

JOHN PIPER

The Perfect Example!

*I have given you an example, that you also
should do just as I have done to you.*

JOHN 13:15 ESV

It is often difficult to find good examples to follow. Even the people we admire most can let us down with their behavior. In today's culture, it is a challenge to find role models, but that truth should remind us that there is only one perfect example to follow. And the place where we experience Him, again and again, is in the Bible.

One day Jesus was washing the disciples' feet after a long day of walking on dusty roads. After taking care of this mundane task, He suggested to the disciples that they "do just as I have done." Jesus was teaching how to be a servant to others in their moments of need.

Serving someone means recognizing his or her importance or significance to us. It means that your interest is primarily focused on what is best for the other person (Philippians 2:3–4). This creates goodwill, comfort, and pleasure toward others, and it is a good or righteous deed.

Jesus modeled the life of service for us in so many ways. Think of when He came upon a woman being accused by others and immediately defused the situation (John 8:1–11). When He spoke in defense of her, her many accusers left without complaint. By studying the example of Jesus in the Bible and learning about what our Savior said and did, we are given eternal lessons on how to treat people. After all, Jesus is the perfect role model!

Father, help me see the needs of people around me. Help me show them that I consider them to be important. Let me love them as You would love them. Help me follow Your perfect example.

*It is by serving God and others
that we store up heavenly treasures.
Everyone gains; no one loses.*

RANDY ALCORN

Your Scars
Are Proof of Life

[Jesus] said to Thomas,
"Put your finger here; see my hands.
Reach out your hand and put it into my side.
Stop doubting and believe."

JOHN 20:27 NIV

Maybe you can identify with my story. The knife in my back from a trusted friend broke more than skin—it broke my heart. Just thinking about how my life unraveled in that moment can still make me nauseous. I am not the same person I was before that wound. Does this sound familiar? Being hurt is unfortunately just part of life—we all experience some form of pain. But when times like this come, remember that Jesus experienced the same pain and carried those scars because He knew that one day you and I would have them too.

Most people hide their scars, but not our Lord. His scars proved to Thomas that He was still alive! In the same way, your scars are evidence that what should have killed you did not. They aren't meant to remind you of the pain you endured. Rather, your scars are a testimony of strength. Always remember that dead men don't scar;

they rot. Scars are signs of the body healing—they are your proof of life!

When Jesus stood among His disciples after the resurrection, He didn't keep His hands in His pockets to conceal the nail imprints. His scars and what they represented were now a permanent part of Him. Keep in mind that it wasn't His voice or His calm, easy manner that Thomas recognized. No, it was nail marks scarring His hands that caused Thomas to believe again!

Your scars can produce the same response in others. So often the difficulties you experience can also highlight the redemptive message of the cross. Just like with Jesus, your scars can proclaim to others, "Do not be afraid." The sorrow and misfortune of your past when surrendered to God can become a healed mark—a beautiful scar. Jesus used His scars to help a doubting man believe. Don't waste what you have been through. Go find a Thomas and show him your scars!

Dear God, heal my injured heart and use the scars of my past to help others stop doubting and start believing.

Don't hide your scars.
Wear them as proof that God heals.

JARRID WILSON

We're Not
Spring Chickens

Even to your old age, I am He,
and even to gray hairs I will carry you!
I have made, and I will bear;
even I will carry, and will deliver you.

ISAIAH 46:4 NKJV

I had a birthday about a month ago and I am well past fifty. I have plantar fasciitis in my left foot, a painful condition that makes it hard to walk sometimes. A couple of weeks ago, an issue with my right knee arose, and after an examination and X-rays, I was diagnosed with arthritis in that knee. A year or so ago, I tore a meniscus in my other knee. I would love to say I was playing basketball or doing something heroic like saving a kitten from a tree, but the truth is I was only trying to get up out of my recliner! Right and left, I am facing the pain of aging these days.

Getting old is not for the weak at heart, but I'm glad God still extends His grace to me. He sticks with me even though I am no longer a "spring chicken." Through the aches and pains and new challenges, He is there, comforting me and continuing to use me. I often offer a prayer of thankfulness that He still believes in me, even though I can no longer get down on my knees to pray.

Lord, thank You for nourishing my inner man even though the wear and tear of aging is evident in my physical body. Continue to use me for Your glory.

One lesson [of aging] is to remind us of our responsibility to be diligent in our service for God right now. I may not be able to do everything I once did (nor does God expect me to), but I am called to be faithful to what I can do. Another lesson surely is to make us realize in a fuller way that this world is not our final home. If our hope truly is in Christ, we are pilgrims in this world, en route to our eternal home in Heaven.

BILLY GRAHAM

His Way Is the Best Way

My thoughts are not your thoughts,
neither are your ways my ways, declares the LORD.

ISAIAH 55:8 ESV

Do you remember asking your father for something and when he said no, going immediately to ask your mother? When your parents were in agreement, they wouldn't budge!

Sometimes we behave as if God works and thinks like we do. But God operates on an omniscient level—His ways and thoughts are superior to ours. Sometimes when we feel that our prayers go unanswered, we need to remember that God, much like our parents, always knows what is best for us. That is why His ways work for good (Romans 8:28). Our ways are usually hit-and-miss at best.

Scripture tells us that the Lord does *whatever* pleases Him (see Psalms 115:3; 135:6). The Bible helps us understand God and His ways, what He says and how He goes about His business. God desires that we succeed in what we do and how we live. He has sent the Holy Spirit to help us in our weakness. Just like our parents did what was best for us when we were young, our heavenly Father's thoughts are always on what is best for us!

Father, help me seek Your thoughts and Your ways in my life today. Help me remember that even when I feel that my prayers go unanswered, You know what is best for me.

There are only two ways to live your life.
One is as though nothing is a miracle.
The other is as though everything is a miracle.

ALBERT EINSTEIN

Bear with Me

Be strong and of good courage, do not fear
nor be afraid of them; for the LORD your God,
He is the One who goes with you.
He will not leave you nor forsake you.

DEUTERONOMY 31:6 NKJV

In the mountains of eastern Kentucky where I live, we pride ourselves in being the Black Bear Capital of the state. The signs entering our communities have cute pictures of these animals on them. My town hosts the Kentucky Black Bear Festival each year, and even the local high school sports teams are known as the Black Bears. It is not unusual to see one of these beautiful-yet-slightly-scary creatures roaming the countryside, climbing trees, or looking for food in people's garbage cans.

This morning as I was driving to work, a baby bear crossed the road right in front of me. I slowed down to give it plenty of time to cross, and then I proceeded carefully with a watchful eye. In my neck of the woods, we have learned that when you see a baby bear, its momma or poppa cannot be too far behind. Bears are fiercely protective of their young and follow them everywhere they go.

In my walk with God, His protection is an ever-present form of grace. When fear strikes, I can speak His name and feel Him near. When I am lonely, I am reminded He is always with me. Even when I stray from His presence at times, like that errant baby bear crossing the street, He pursues me and leads me back home.

Father, how wonderful it is that You never let Your guard down and You are always protecting me. I praise You for Your ever-present attention to me.

At their core, when things really matter, people see a need to turn to God for strength and protection.

LEE GREENWOOD

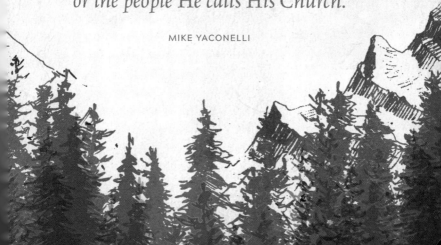

*T*he grace of God is dangerous.
It's lavish, excessive, outrageous,
and scandalous. God's grace is ridiculously
inclusive. Apparently God doesn't care
who He loves. He is not very careful
about the people He calls His friends
or the people He calls His Church.

MIKE YACONELLI

Racing to Win . . .
Together

Though one may be overpowered,
two can defend themselves.
A cord of three strands is not quickly broken.

ECCLESIASTES 4:12 NIV

Each summer the world watches as some of the toughest athletes on the globe gather in Europe for the Tour de France. This grueling test of endurance stretches over 2,200 miles in twenty-one days of racing and covers some of the steepest terrain on the continent. Between twenty and twenty-two riders, each supported by a team of bicyclists, vigorously compete for top honors. All who finish the race are victors, but to receive the coveted trophy is the absolute pinnacle of bicycle racing.

What many do not realize is that each racer's teammates surround and insulate him from bumps that could cost him the race. They help break the air in front, protect from possible crashes on each side, and pace the lead biker appropriately. They even sacrifice their own bodies and race times in order to benefit the leader.

Every man needs his own team to surround and support him as well. Instead of attacking life solo and wondering why we fail, let's recognize the benefits of helping each other complete life's race. That trek often includes steep climbs, sharp curves, and some exciting downhill stretches. Nevertheless, the journey is more enjoyable, and we are more likely to finish it well, if we have a committed team around us.

Overcoming life's adversities is more rewarding than all the prize money in the world. Just as a Tour winner traditionally share his winnings with his team, so, too, should we share with our "teammates" in life the joy of victory when the race is completed. So let's surround and help each other finish strong!

Father, gather around me a strong team so that we might run our race well together.

Friendship is one of the sweetest joys of life. Many might have failed beneath the bitterness of their trial had they not found a friend.

CHARLES H. SPURGEON

In a League of Our Own

As iron sharpens iron,
so a friend sharpens a friend.

PROVERBS 27:17 NLT

I have been playing recreational softball on the same team for fifteen years. The average age of our roster is . . . let's say more *mature* than any of the other teams in the league. We are a scrappy bunch that prides ourselves on playing good, fundamental defense, and as a result—much to the chagrin and often to the surprise of our opponents—we win many more games than we lose.

We are made up of a beautiful cross section of culture, race, and gender represented by a variety of different religious backgrounds and political beliefs. We enjoy spending time together, and even though we don't always agree on everything, it doesn't affect our play when we take the field. "Play for the name on the front of the jersey, not the one on the back" is the motto we strive to apply as an integral part of our strategy.

We know that we can count on each other off the field as well. If one of us needs to move, the others are there to help with the heavy lifting. I was in a serious car accident ten years ago, and this band of brothers and sisters was at my hospital bedside, carefully navigating the stitches and bruises as they shaved my face and washed the blood from my hair. Last year I even had the incredible privilege of officiating the wedding of two of my teammates who fell in love on the diamond.

Though they may not even be aware of it, I often see Jesus in the kindness, thoughtfulness, and unselfishness that bind my ball-playing friends to one another. I have come to appreciate that the unique qualities I experience when I am in their company assure me that I will always have more wins than losses on and off the field—no matter what the final scoreboard says.

God, I am grateful for the great groups of friends that You have blessed me with. Help me always be patient with those I care about, and let me always be mindful that our differences can be used in ways that unite us rather than divide us.

Diversity is the one thing we all have in common. Celebrate it every day.

UNKNOWN

Giving Life with a Name

*Adam named his wife Eve, because she would
become the mother of all the living.*

GENESIS 3:20 NIV

Before the fall, Adam's wife was simply called "woman." After the fall, when Adam had the task of naming her, he called her Eve. In the original Hebrew, the name he gave her was *chawwah*, or "life." That's right, even after they had sinned, Adam named his wife "life." While Adam and Eve were aware of God's instructions regarding the forbidden fruit (Genesis 2:17), I truly believe neither of them expected such severe long-term consequences. If Eve had known we would still be paying the tab, she might not have ordered such a lavish meal.

Like Adam, God has given you the power to give a name or "title" to those who have messed up. When we are hurt by the actions of others, it puts us in a position to permanently label them. Perhaps you have the name tag already prepared for someone who has made a choice that has hurt you. But have you considered the name God would have you assign them? Maybe they aren't as bad as you have made them out to be, and maybe you, like Adam, share some responsibility in the mess.

Jesus always prayed for His enemies. With one sentence Adam had the power not only to demonstrate forgiveness but to also heal Eve's wounded heart. I can hear her now: "After all I've done, and he called me 'life'!" Whom do you need to give a different name? Today, decide to be like Adam by refusing to allow the mistakes others have made in the past to become their permanent identity—that is, after all, what God has done for you.

Dear God, regardless of their response, I release forgiveness to those who have intentionally or unintentionally hurt me. I choose to speak life over them and not death.

To be a Christian means to forgive the inexcusable, because God has forgiven the inexcusable in you.

C. S. LEWIS

You Are Not Forsaken

At the ninth hour Jesus cried with a loud voice,
"Eloi, Eloi, lema sabachthani?" which means,
"My God, my God, why have you forsaken me?"

MARK 15:34 ESV

When a thunderstorm knocks the power out and darkness invades my home, the first thing I do is locate my sons. When they were little, finding them was much easier. All I had to do was follow the sound of cries for rescue. "Daddy, we can't see," echoed up and down the hallway. My presence during darkness meant more to them than my being there when the lights were on.

I've heard it said that at the cross God turned His back on Jesus, leaving Him all alone in His darkest hour. I, however, am not convinced. Could it be that we have mistaken God's timing for God's absence? The darkness was the culprit. Remember, God can see you even when you can't see Him. It is impossible for Him to turn His back on you. I believe God never lost sight of Jesus on the cross, and in the very same way God will never lose sight of you! Remember, you can't trust your feelings when the lights go out.

The psalmist David said it best: "Then I said to myself, 'Oh he even sees me in the dark! At night I am immersed in light!' It's a fact: darkness isn't dark to you; night and day, darkness and light, they're all the same to you" (Psalm 139:11–12 MSG). Relax. In these times you only need to worship and seek His face. You can trust your heavenly Father with the future. He loves you too much to disappoint you. You are not forsaken.

Dear God, even when I can't see You, help me understand that You are vigilantly watching over me.

Every time that you feel forsaken,
every time that you feel alone,
He is near to the broken hearted,
every tear He knows.

JEREMY CAMP

Embrace the Seasons of Life

Every good gift and every perfect gift is from above,
and comes down from the Father of lights,
with whom there is no variation or shadow of turning.

JAMES 1:17 NKJV

My wife and I visited our sons at college one weekend, and we had a good time catching up over lunch. Since the boys first left home, our nest has been empty and our life has changed. Instead of cooking a big supper every night, we do takeout or prepare smaller meals. Our food budget has shrunk, as has the amount of laundry we do each week. It has been an adjustment, to say the least.

At times I get wistful when I see social media posts from friends whose children are still at home. These mothers and fathers are chasing their young ones through various activities: a cross-country meet at a far locale, a tennis match on the home courts, a track meet that lasts all day. I once walked in those parents' shoes, but that part of my life is effectively over.

There are times I miss the hustle and bustle, the travel, and those seemingly endless track meets. This transition in our lives has caused my wife and me to feel lost, not knowing what to do with the newfound time on our hands.

When I feel down, missing my boys, I remember God designed our world for seasons and for change. I believe it's that way so we will cling to the One constant in life. Seasons come and go, but the Bible tells me Jesus Christ remains the same yesterday, today, and forever (Hebrews 13:8). When change comes, He gives me grace to withstand it so I can continue to follow Him.

Father, help me embrace the seasons of life and the changes they bring. Help me cling to You, the unchanging One.

The world has changed
and it's going to keep changing,
but God never changes;
so we are safe when we cling to Him.

CHARLES R. SWINDOLL

Grace does not depend on

what we have done for God

but rather what God has done for us.

Ask people what they must do to get

to heaven and most reply, "Be good."

Jesus's stories contradict that answer.

All we must do is cry, "Help!"

PHILIP YANCEY

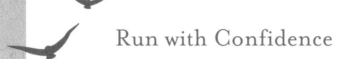

Run with Confidence

The LORD will go before you,
the God of Israel will be your rear guard.

ISAIAH 52:12 NIV

I have always loved football. When I was growing up, I enjoyed watching and reading about the great running backs of the NFL. Larry Csonka, Jim Brown, Gale Sayers, Franco Harris, and others lit up my imagination and inspired many fantasy front-yard touchdowns. Many of the records left behind by these great competitors have since been outdone by younger and faster athletes with better training and superior equipment, but these heroes of the past will always hold hallowed spots in my memory.

Most of the great NFL running backs, however, will tell you that their success depended entirely on their blockers. Although their athleticism, quick judgment, and agility enhanced their performance, no amount of fancy footwork and power could overcome consistently missed blocks. The best running backs attacked the defense with an inner confidence and reliance on the skills of their linemen.

It's a blessing to understand we have someone "blocking" for us in life. God, as He did with Israel, promises to lead the way before us—and He even assures us that He's got our back as well! Whenever we face difficult days with employers, peers, or foes, it's empowering to know we're not alone and that we don't have to grind out those difficult yards under our own power. We can run with confidence and assurance on the gridiron of life, knowing that God is clearing our path.

Dear God, thank You for preparing the way for me today and for watching my back. Help me run faithfully.

*The LORD himself goes before you and will be with you;
he will never leave you nor forsake you.
Do not be afraid; do not be discouraged.*

DEUTERONOMY 31:8 NIV

Workin' for a Livin'

The glory of young men is their strength,
and the splendor of old men is their gray head.

PROVERBS 20:29 NKJV

I am a teacher by trade and used to believe my job would get easier with experience. Boy, was I wrong. I have been in the same position for over twenty-five years, and the last few have been some of the toughest of my career. Times have changed in education, like any other profession, with advanced technology, new methods of delivery, and students who have ever-decreasing attention spans. It is enough to make an old dog like me want to roll over and take a nap rather than learn new tricks. I have always been the type of guy to go with the flow, but lately the flow has threatened to whisk me away in the current!

When I first decided to follow Jesus twenty years ago, I expected the Christian life to be the same—I thought my walk would get easier as time passed and I gained experience. Instead, I have found this journey *more* challenging the farther down the road I travel this side of heaven.

I have found grace in the truth that the older we get, the more we rely on God. When I was younger, I tended to falter by trusting my own abilities to address the challenges of work and life. But as I have aged, I've learned to lean on God for the strength to make it through each day. God's grace is sweeter as we learn to depend on Him more and more on this heaven-bound journey.

Lord, today please make me aware of my need for Your grace as I do Your work in this world.

God is still at work through the hundreds of thousands of gifted teachers and administrators, committed parents, and passionate volunteers who seek to help give our children "a future with hope."

ADAM HAMILTON

God Isn't
a Fair-Weather Fan

*You, O LORD, are a God full of compassion,
and gracious, longsuffering and abundant
in mercy and truth.*

PSALM 86:15 NKJV

I live in Kentucky and cheer for the Wildcats, known for their elite basketball tradition. Even though I love the accomplishments on the hardwood, I also follow the University of Kentucky's football team, which hasn't enjoyed the same level of success.

The Kentucky football team lost to Florida again recently, and this particular ending was difficult to watch. They led the whole game until the final minute, when the Gators scored the winning touchdown for the school's thirty-first straight win over my Wildcats. I was shocked and upset, but that is nothing new for a longtime UK football fan.

Every football season I get frustrated during the Kentucky losses and vow not to follow the team anymore. Call me a "true blue" fan or a glutton for punishment, but I always find myself parked back in front of the television when the next game rolls around. After all, college football enthusiasts in our state have endured so many disappointing finishes to games over the years that I think we embody the definition of *long-suffering*. But you know something? All these disappointments actually make the occasional victories even more special! In the long run, I think it's safe to say I will never be a fair-weather fan of my football team.

I realized recently that God is not a fair-weather fan either. I bet at times I have caused Him a whole lot more frustration than what I feel watching football on Saturdays in my home state, but He never gives up on me. I make mistakes daily . . . sometimes hourly . . . yet He sticks with me, teaching me lessons through my errors and encouraging me to move on. When I blow it and feel defeated—like the Wildcats allowing another last-minute touchdown—He is ever-present, extending His grace and mercy and cheering me on no matter what!

Father, I praise You for being long-suffering toward me and for loving me through the mistakes and bad days.

What gives me the most hope every day is God's grace; knowing that his grace is going to give me the strength for whatever I face, knowing that nothing is a surprise to God.

RICK WARREN

God Is Always at Work

How then can I do this great wickedness,
and sin against God?

GENESIS 39:9 NKJV

Potiphar's wife tempted Joseph, and while it would have been easy for him to take advantage of the situation, he stayed focused on obeying God. Things didn't turn out well for Joseph when the Pharaoh's wife, spurned by his rejection, accused him of wrongdoing. Joseph was thrown in prison, but God was at work on something much greater behind the scenes.

Joseph found himself dependent upon the good word of others if he was ever to be freed. So he began to interpret dreams for people in the hope that it might lead to him being released from prison. Eventually the king had a dream that defied explanation, and Joseph was brought before him to interpret it. He was not only released from prison but elevated to a position of power because he remained faithful to God even in suffering.

The king placed Joseph second in command over all of Egypt—exactly where God wanted him. Remember that God was working through all of Joseph's seeming misfortune to put him in the only position that could allow him to rescue his family from a coming famine.

Even when things may have seemed hopeless to Joseph, God was remaining faithful. We can also live with the expectation that God is working behind the scenes to accomplish great things through us. Even when it seems everything is going wrong, stay faithful to God, and you will be surprised by the outcome!

Father, help me see the big picture as You work in my life. Let me expect the unexpected, always giving thanks, praise, and honor to Your name. Help me remember today that You are always at work—whether I can see it or not.

Every time I say "no" to a small temptation, I strengthen my will to say "no" to a greater one.

MOTHER ANGELICA

Our Good Father

*If you, then, though you are evil,
know how to give good gifts to your children,
how much more will your Father in heaven give
good gifts to those who ask him!*

MATTHEW 7:11 NIV

Imagine, for a moment, the scene of a dad wrestling on the floor with his six-year-old son. The boy is overwhelmed with giggling, and that laughter is rising as the dad tickles him. The son reciprocates by attempting to tickle his dad. The joy on the father's face is unmistakable, and it is obvious *there is no place else* he would rather be!

The Bible teaches us that God is our Father in heaven. It also explains that when we see a "good father" on earth, it is a reflection of the truth that God is *truly* our good Father. As men, many of us have an easy time seeing God as holy, good, and just. But God's love and His enjoyment of us as His children can be harder to comprehend.

God's Word teaches us that whatever "good" looks like for man pales in comparison to how our Father in heaven loves us. The description of a dad playing with his son is a joyful, good moment of earthly fatherhood. God wants us to know that He loves us *more* and desires to bring us even greater joy than the father in the scene I described.

God *never* stops loving us. Even in our worst moments, our Father in heaven dotes on us. We may pull away from Him, but He will never leave us or forsake us.

Father, help me know Your love and believe that You *love* me and delight to give me good gifts and to bring me unspeakable joy!

*Don't we all long for a father who, even though
our mistakes are written all over the wall,
will love us anyway? Don't we want a father who cares for us
in spite of our failures? We do have that type of a father.
A father who is at his best when we are at our worst.
A father whose grace is strongest
when our devotion is weakest.*

MAX LUCADO

I am not what I ought to be.

I am not what I want to be.

I am not what I hope to be.

But still, I am not what I used to be.

And by the grace of God,

I am what I am.

JOHN NEWTON

The Outcome
Has Been Decided

*You were dead because of your sins and because
your sinful nature was not yet cut away.
Then God made you alive with Christ, for he forgave
all our sins. He canceled the record of the charges
against us and took it away by nailing it to the cross.*

COLOSSIANS 2:13–14 NLT

One reason men love sports is because of the presence of a scoreboard. We like to know who has won and who has lost. It's that simple. Our world is filled with ambiguity and relativism, and sports are an ever-present haven from this uncertainty. We can sit down and watch a game and be clear on who is ahead, who is behind, and who is ultimately the victor of the contest.

Our Father in heaven wants us to have even more certainty as we face the challenges of life on earth. He has already let us know the final score. When Jesus took our sins upon Himself, God's wrath was poured out on Him who knew no sin. As a result, the enemy has already been vanquished.

Sometimes sports commentators will discuss how a team with a track record of losing will have to *learn to win*. In essence, these teams are so used to losing that even when they start to play better, they may revert to old behaviors and habits because they haven't accepted the habits of winning. But God has shown us the final score so that we can begin to live confidently—so that we can play the game of life like winners. Because we already know the outcome of this great struggle, we can live a life of repentance, relying on the Holy Spirit to empower us to live obedient, victorious lives.

Father, I praise You for Your power and victory as You defeated sin through the cross and death through Christ's victory over the grave. Help me live a life of repentance and obedience as I rely on Your Holy Spirit.

As a result of grace, we have been saved from sin's penalty.
One day we will be saved from sin's presence.
In the meantime we are being saved from sin's power.

ALISTAIR BEGG

Killing Lions
in Snowy Pits

There was . . . Benaiah son of Jehoiada,
a valiant warrior from Kabzeel.
He did many heroic deeds, which included killing
two champions of Moab. Another time, on a snowy day,
he chased a lion down into a pit and killed it.

2 SAMUEL 23:20 NLT

Benaiah was a man's man. In the listing of King David's mighty warriors, he commanded special respect not only for his spectacular victories over notable human foes but also for his conquest of a lion in a pit on a snowy day!

Killing a lion without a firearm in and of itself deserves special mention, but to do so when traction and agility have been compromised by a layer of slippery snow makes the task much more incredible. Add the fact that this battle was not fought in the open country but in the confines of some pit, and it is a superb act of valor and bravery indeed. Such a conquest deserves all the recognition he receives in the pages of the Old Testament.

What lions do you face? Sometimes we all encounter adversaries that seem to have an advantage. Our odds of coming out of our pits victorious are less than those afforded Jehoiada's son. It may be a pit of addiction to pornography, work, or a destructive substance. It may be a problem with diet or exercise. Overcoming it seems impossible, and so we often never try. Instead of risking another failure, we resign ourselves to defeat in the snowy pit.

I challenge you to take courage from Benaiah and renew your battle. Realize that you are not fighting it alone, but that the Commander of the Lord's army fights with you and for you. Take up His armor and weapons and engage the enemy. And don't hesitate to use the helpful tools the Father offers you in the form of professional counselors, praying pastors, and accountability groups. With God's help, we can slay our lions in spite of the snow and the pits.

Dear Jesus, fight my lions for me and with me.

The battle is the LORD's.

1 SAMUEL 17:47 NIV

A Gateway to Grace

We have this treasure in earthen vessels,
that the excellence of the power
may be of God, and not of us.

2 CORINTHIANS 4:7 NKJV

I was an overachiever throughout my formative years. I got straight As in high school, and mostly As and Bs in college—we won't mention geography or physical science—and a near-perfect record, with one B, in graduate school. I mention all of this not to brag but to highlight my perfectionist tendencies.

Recently I tried something new in the class I teach in children's church, and it did not go well. Fidgeting and trying to hit each other, the youngsters were less interested in the lesson and more concerned with snack time. Despite all my hard work, the lesson for that Sunday was a total failure.

Because of my perfectionism, failure doesn't sit well with me. When something I attempt doesn't go as planned—which happens more often than I'd like to admit—I am my own worst enemy. I beat myself up, replaying all the things that went wrong and overanalyzing what I could have done differently to change the outcome. But after that disastrous class with the children,

God gave me a revelation: I had tried to do that lesson on my own strength, not in His.

God not only wants me to learn from my mistakes, but He also wants me to depend solely on Him, to offer up my weaknesses. That level of surrender does not come easily to someone who was raised as an only child, independent and overachieving from an early age, but I now know His grace is extended in a special way when I give Him control.

In those times when I mess up in my own efforts, God's mercy and power become more evident as I try again in His strength. *Fail* does not have to be a four-letter bad word; it can be our gateway to God's grace.

Father, help me learn from my mistakes and operate in Your strength, not in mine.

Failures, repeated failures, are finger posts on the road to achievement. One fails forward toward success.

C. S. LEWIS

Closer Than a Brother

*One who has unreliable friends soon comes to ruin,
but there is a friend who sticks closer than a brother.*

PROVERBS 18:24 NIV

Several years ago, I went through a particularly dark time in my life. Someone I had loved and devoted myself to abandoned me, and suddenly my entire world was turned upside down. During those long, difficult months, God became more real to me than ever. As I immersed myself in the Psalms, He spoke His love and assurance to me in deep and wonderful ways.

It was also during this time that I really learned to pray. Although my parents taught me this important spiritual discipline as a child, the depth of need and hunger for His intimacy brought me closer to God than I'd ever been before.

But God also gave me another special gift. He gave me a friend. I will be forever grateful to the spiritual brother who became a constant source of encouragement and help. His phone calls were a lifeline, and he was willing to talk any time of the day or night. He listened to me complain and was there to bring me some much-needed perspective. Whenever I talked of doing things that would hurt myself (or others), he was faithfully present to talk me off the ledge.

I'm very thankful for the gift of a friend that God provided. If it hadn't been for my friend who stuck to me closer than a brother during that time, I'm not sure where I'd be today. If God has given you such a friend, thank Him. If not, ask Him to reveal who that person is in your life, and be intentional about being such a friend to someone else.

Father, thank You for Your presence in dark times and for providing friends to walk with me through those moments.

I have called you friends, for everything that I learned from my Father I have made known to you.

JOHN 15:15 NIV

Make Up Your Mind

Daniel resolved that he would not defile himself.

DANIEL 1:8 ESV

Daniel (who was a teenager at the time) *made up his mind* about food and drink. He determined out of his personal convictions and the Word of God what he could eat and what he would not eat (Leviticus 11:47). The king chose young men to serve him and wanted them to have the best food and drink. All of the other young servants chose to eat the king's food.

But many of those chosen foods had been offered to idols, and Daniel felt he would be breaking a personal moral code to partake of the offerings to idols. He felt it would defile him spiritually, and he was committed to obeying his God. He and a few of his friends stood firm in their decision, regardless of the consequences they may face.

Furthermore, Daniel challenged the system by stating that he and his friends would be healthier than those who ate the king's food (Daniel 1:18–20). After many days, it was evident that Daniel's convictions made an impact on those observing the young men. God blessed Daniel. Daniel proved to be righteous in his standing before God, before his own people, and before the people who held him captive. And God honored his obedience.

God is looking for men who will take a stand for what is holy, a decision that will not always be popular, but one that is pleasing to Him. Set your sights on the work of God in your life and it will show those around you that God is at work in you!

Father, teach me Your Word so that I can obey it. Give me courage and strength to keep and obey all You want me to accomplish.

We have a choice every day regarding the attitude we will embrace for that day.

CHARLES R. SWINDOLL

If we are saved by grace alone,
this salvation is a constant source
of amazed delight. Nothing is mundane
or matter-of-fact about our lives.
It is a miracle we are Christians,
and the Gospel, which creates
bold humility, should give us
a far deeper sense of humor and joy.
We don't take ourselves seriously,
and we are full of hope for the world.

TIM KELLER

Avoid the Prevent Defense

Don't you realize that in a race everyone runs,
but only one person gets the prize?
So run to win!

1 CORINTHIANS 9:24 NLT

Up two touchdowns with seven minutes left in the game and as your team begins lining up three on the line and backing up the secondary and linebackers . . . you realize that it is the dreaded prevent defense! This defensive alignment is so reviled by many fans that it is referred to as the "prevent victory defense."

The prevent defense is a good thing when there are only minutes or seconds left in a game, but if it's implemented too early, the problem with the prevent defense is that it takes a team away from the things that had captured the lead in the first place. Often the team stops playing to win and begins playing *not to lose*. The idea behind a prevent defense is to prevent the opposing offense from making big plays. When a defense does this and there is still a lot of time on the clock, it usually ends up allowing the opponent to make small advances down the field.

The enemy of our soul wants us to play this very same type of prevent defense. He wants to steal, kill, and destroy. Jesus came that we might have life and have it more abundantly. The enemy wants us to look around and fear what we may lose. He wants us to live our lives "not to lose." But Jesus wants us to know that we *cannot* lose as long as we trust in Him. As the apostle Paul exhorted the Corinthians, we are meant to run to win!

Father, forgive me for giving in to my fears. Help me live confident, not of myself but in Your love, power, and victory over the enemy.

Let this certainty [of God being for you] make its impact on you in relation to what you are up against at this very moment, and you will find in thus knowing God as your sovereign protector, irrevocably committed to you in the covenant of grace, both freedom from fear and new strength for the fight.

J. I. PACKER

Carried by God

But now, O Lord, you are our Father;
we are the clay, and you are our potter;
we are all the work of your hand.

ISAIAH 64:8 ESV

A friend of mine faces a daily battle against deep emotional and psychological issues that have been a part of his life since childhood. Counseling and pastoral care have helped him meet the challenges with varying degrees of success, but he has recently discovered that pairing therapy with his gift for creating art has been the best path to emotional healing and spiritual wellness.

His art is intensely personal, and it is often a reflection of the core of who he is. His colorful, dramatic drawings communicate in ways that he finds extremely difficult to express with words. Like many artists, he prefers that his works speak through the viewers' individual interpretations so that they might find a glimpse of themselves in his creations.

Three years ago, he discovered the biblical meaning of his name, which resonated deeply with him. For most of his life, he had been shamed by the burden of negative self-talk and wounded by the labels and stereotypes that others had placed on him. He decided to make it a permanent and visible reminder by having this name tattooed on his forearm. The permanently inked "Carried by God" is now the enduring assurance of who he is through the eyes of his Creator, and it also covers a landscape of scars that had accumulated from years of self-mutilation. For much of his life he only wore long-sleeved shirts to keep his secrets hidden. Now, even in the bitter cold of winter, he wears t-shirts so that everyone knows exactly who and, more importantly, whose he is!

Abba, thank You for seeing me for who I really am underneath my own shame and scars. Your death and the gift of Your redemption are free and everlasting reminders that I am, have always been, and will always be Your beloved.

*It's like a soul tattoo . . .
love like this will never fade away.*

MARGARET BECKER

Take a Hike!

As for me, it is good to be near God.
I have made the Sovereign LORD my refuge;
I will tell of all your deeds.

PSALM 73:28 NIV

Every year we all see the magazine headlines touting the unexpected health benefits of walking or hiking. It boosts your creativity! Improves sleep! Slashes stress! Curbs the sweet tooth! There is a two-mile trail close to where I live that, at least in this case, makes me believe that everything I read really is true.

My favorite way to walk this trail is to start at a spot that begins with groves of cedar trees that allow plenty of sunlight to shine through on a beautiful day. But as the trail continues deeper into the wild, it leads to an old-growth Tennessee forest made up of huge trees with prehistoric-sized trunks and vast canopies that let in enough light to see but are so thick that they have managed to keep me completely dry in an unexpected downpour. Sometimes I attempt to hum a song of praise as I walk, pausing often to listen to the cacophony of sounds from the birds and bugs. I try to identify some of the trees by looking closely at their leaves or the nuts or fruits that fall from them. If

I am especially lucky I might spot a deer, a woodpecker, a snake, a hawk, or a fox.

I never, ever leave the forest without feeling more centered, settled, moved, and inspired . . . especially when I experience the trail on a solo hike. More often than not I feel like I have all 136 acres to myself. But by God's incredible mystery, even when I am alone I feel like I am a part of something bigger. I am humbled by the realization that I am part of His great masterpiece. Being surrounded by the awesomeness of His creation makes me feel bound to Him in powerful and profound ways.

Father God, thank You for reminding me that You are always near and that my life has meaning and purpose. Help me open my eyes so that I am able to see You everywhere I go.

It is not so much for its beauty that the forest makes a claim upon men's hearts, as for that subtle something, that quality of air that emanation from old trees, that so wonderfully changes and renews a weary spirit.

ROBERT LOUIS STEVENSON

Amazing grace!

How sweet the sound,

that saved a wretch like me!

I once was lost but now am found,

was blind but now I see.

JOHN NEWTON